FINANCIAL HARMONY: NAVIGATING WEALTH WITH WISDOM AND WELLNESS

Contents

4

Prologue to the Brain research of Cash

Section 1: Characterizing the Territory

1.1 The Convergence of Cash and Brain research

Investigating the complicated connection among cash and the human brain.

Perceiving the mental elements that shape monetary ways of behaving.

1.2 The Meaning of Figuring out Cash Brain research

Examining the reason why a profound comprehension of the brain research of cash is vital.

Featuring the effect of mental variables on monetary prosperity.

Section 2: Feelings and Cash

2.1 Feelings as Monetary Drivers

Analyzing the job of feelings in molding monetary choices.

Recognizing the profound triggers that impact cash related ways of behaving.

2.2 Ability to appreciate people at their core in Money

Presenting the idea of the ability to appreciate people on a deeper level with regards to individual budget.

Methodologies for developing profound mindfulness and guideline in monetary issues.

Part 3: Mental Inclinations and Monetary Independent direction

3.1 Unwinding Mental Predispositions

Grasping normal mental predispositions that influence monetary decisions.

Delineating how predispositions can prompt poor monetary results.

3.2 Exploring the Mental Minefield

Viable methods for perceiving and moderating mental predispositions in monetary navigation.

Contextual analyses featuring the effect of mental predispositions on cash related decisions.

Section 4: Conduct Financial matters Focal point

4.1 Prologue to Conduct Financial matters

Investigating key standards of conduct financial matters and their importance to back.

How social financial aspects challenges customary monetary suppositions.

4.2 Applications in Ordinary Money

Certifiable instances of how social financial matters ideas can be applied to individual budget.

Bits of knowledge into further developing dynamic utilizing

conduct financial matters standards.

This is only a beginning stage, and each segment could dig further into explicit ideas and models. Contingent upon the writer's methodology, the presentation could likewise incorporate tales, contextual analyses, or viable activities to draw in peruses in pondering their own monetary ways of behaving.

Cash and Feelings

Part 1: The Emotional Landscape of Finance

1.1 The Emotional Rollercoaster

Investigating the highs and lows of emotions in financial circumstances

Understanding the close to home unpredictability related with cash.

1.2 Profound Triggers in Monetary Direction

Distinguishing normal close to home triggers that impact monetary decisions.

how emotions can affect long-term financial goals and cloud judgment.

Section 2: Dread and Eagerness in Money

2.1 Apprehension: The Loss of motion Component

Looking at how dread can block normal dynamic in monetary issues.

Methodologies for overseeing and defeating dread notwithstanding monetary difficulties.

2.2 Greed: The Enticement of Overabundance

Figuring out the job of avarice in hazardous monetary way of behaving.

Offsetting desire with mindful monetary independent direction.

Part 3: The ability to understand people at their core and Monetary Health

3.1 The Job of The ability to understand people on a deeper level

Characterizing the ability to understand people on a deeper level with regards to monetary prosperity.

How the ability to appreciate individuals on a deeper level adds to pursuing sound monetary decisions.

3.2 Cultivating Emotional Resilience

Steps to take to cultivate emotional resilience in difficult financial circumstances

forming a mentality that is able to cope with financial ups and downs.

Section 4: Close to home Spending and Saving

4.1 The Drive to Spend

Dissecting the close to home drivers behind rash spending.

methods for reducing emotional spending patterns.

4.2 The Test of Saving

Unwinding close to home hindrances to setting aside cash.

establishing an emotional connection to the act of saving that is positive.

Part 5: Emotional Implications of Financial Objectives

5.1 Establishing Emotionally Resonant Objectives Aligning personal values and objectives with financial objectives.

The persuasive force of sincerely charged monetary targets.

5.2 Adapting to Objective Related Pressure

Perceiving and overseeing pressure related with monetary objective pursuit.

Offsetting aspiration with taking care of oneself chasing monetary goals.

This chapter delves into the psychological factors that influence financial decisions and examines the intricate connection between money and emotions. From the profound rollercoaster of monetary encounters to the effect of dread and avarice, peruses will acquire bits of knowledge into dealing with their feelings for better monetary prosperity. The section likewise underscores the significance of the capacity to understand people on a deeper level and offers reasonable systems for exploring personal difficulties in the domain of individual accounting.

Mental Predispositions in Money

Part 1: Understanding Cognitive Biases

1.1 Through the Eyes of Bias
Defining cognitive biases and the role they play in forming perceptions of finances

Perceiving the unavoidable idea of predispositions in navigation.

1.2 Kinds of Mental Inclinations
Investigating normal mental inclinations pertinent to fund.

how biases influence financial decisions and actions.

Section 2: Mooring and Change

2.1 Mooring in Monetary Navigation
Unloading the idea of mooring and its impact on monetary decisions.

Examples from real life that show how the anchoring effect works.

2.2 Procedures to Moderate Securing

Methods for perceiving and defeating the securing predisposition.

Fostering a more goal way to deal with monetary direction.

Part 3: Misfortune Repugnance

3.1 The Anxiety toward Misfortune

Figuring out the mental effect of misfortune repugnance on monetary choices.

How the apprehension about misfortune can prompt less than ideal decisions.

3.2 Overcoming Loss Aversion

Methods for Controlling and Reducing Loss Aversion

Embracing a decent point of view on hazard and prize.

Section 4: Tendency to look for predictable answers

4.1 Looking for Affirmation

Inspecting the propensity to lean toward data that affirms prior convictions.

How tendency to look for predictable answers can mutilate monetary independent direction.

4.2 Strategies for preventing and combating confirmation bias Breaking the Confirmation Bias Cycle

Developing a liberal way to deal with monetary data.

Part 5: Carelessness Inclination

5.1 The Traps of Pomposity

Investigating the effect of carelessness on monetary gamble taking.

True outcomes of misjudging one's monetary capacities.

5.2 Lowliness in Money

Developing monetary lowliness to balance presumptuousness.

Cooperative ways to deal with direction and chance administration.

Insights Integrating cognitive biases into the broader field of behavioral finance. Behavioral finance and investor behavior

What financial backer way of behaving is meant for by mental predispositions.

6.2 Exploring the Silly Market

Procedures for financial backers to perceive and adjust to nonsensical market ways of behaving.

Long haul points of view for exploring the erratic idea of monetary business sectors.

This part investigates the different mental predispositions that can affect monetary independent direction. From mooring and misfortune repugnance for tendency to look for predetermined feedback and arrogance, peruses will acquire bits of knowledge into the mental elements that might prompt poor monetary decisions. Commonsense systems for perceiving and moderating these predispositions are given, with an emphasis on advancing more levelheaded and objective monetary navigation.

Lead Monetary angles and Money

1.1 The Marriage of Cerebrum science and Monetary issues

Describing conduct monetary matters and its departure from standard money related theories.

comprehending how brain research contributes to financial navigation.

1.2 Key Thoughts in Direct Monetary issues

Layout of fundamental thoughts like heuristics, inclinations, and prospect speculation.

How lead monetary issues hardships the assumptions of outdated monetary issues.

Segment 2: Prospect Speculation and Free heading

2.1 Chance Speculation Basics

Dumping prospect speculation and its ideas for money related free bearing.

Framing and its impact on obvious increments and incidents.

2.2 Applications in Individual bookkeeping

Authentic occurrences of how prospect speculation can go with feeling of individual financial choices.

Frameworks for individuals to investigate dynamic under weakness.

Part 3: Nudges and Choice Plan

3.1 The Power of Nudges

Exploring pushes and their impact on decision results.

Moral thoughts in the usage of knocks in money related settings.

3.2 Arranging Money related Conditions

Applying norms of choice plan to individual financial plan.

How individuals can lay out conditions that help positive financial approaches to acting.

Area 4: Social Monetary matters and Hold reserves

4.1 Social Pieces of information into Saving Approach to acting

Understanding the psychological factors that affect saving affinities.

Trying social financial matters to assist with peopling save more.

4.2 Programmed Enlistment and Default Choices Exploring the viability of programmed enlistment and default choices in retirement reserve funds

Balancing freedom with the benefits of default choices in financial decisions.

Part 5: The Outlandishness of Reasonability

5.1 Prudent Unique Legends

Uncovering dreams about genuine unique in monetary issues.

accepting the reality of human madness and its financial decision-making suggestions.

5.2 Tolerating Limited Levelheadedness

The job of limited objectivity in understanding practical direction are examined.

Systems for making effective decisions within the bounds of human mental capacity.

This segment familiarizes per users with the hypnotizing field of social monetary angles and its application to individual spending plan. The study looks at how mental experiences can change how we interpret financial navigation, from the prospect hypothesis to the use of pushes. Sensible applications and methodology for individuals are included, engaging parsers to ponder the social factors that shape their financial choices.

Cash and Joy

Section 1: The Quest for Bliss

1.1 The Association Among Cash and Prosperity

Looking at the connection between monetary abundance and joy.

introducing the concept and components of subjective well-being.

1.2 The Decadent Treadmill

Understanding the peculiarity where expanded pay may not prompt supported satisfaction.

how the pursuit of happiness is affected by adaptation and comparison.

Section 2: Necessities, Needs, and Satisfaction

2.1 Maslow's Order of Necessities

Investigating how fundamental necessities and higher-request needs add to prosperity.

The job of monetary assets in satisfying different degrees of requirements.

2.2 Past Realism

Assessing the effect of materialistic pursuits on satisfaction.

Methods for achieving happiness that go beyond material possessions.

Part 3: The Financial aspects of Time and Satisfaction

3.1 Time Wealth

The meaning of time chasing after satisfaction.

Adjusting time and cash to upgrade by and large prosperity.

3.2 The Mystery of Time

What the designation of time means for satisfaction.

Time-spending techniques that augment bliss and fulfillment.

Section 4: Cash and Connections

4.1 The Effect of Monetary Weight on Connections

Looking at what monetary tensions can mean for individual connections.

Methodologies for exploring monetary difficulties in associations.

4.2 Shared Encounters and Quality Time

Featuring the job of shared encounters and quality time in relationship satisfaction.

how to put relationships' non-material aspects first.

Part 5: Spending and Joy

5.1 The Delight of Giving

Investigating the connection among liberality and joy.

The mental advantages of expenditure on others.

5.2 Purposeful Spending for Prosperity

How purposeful spending decisions can add to satisfaction.

Making a qualities based going through plan for more prominent time on earth fulfillment.

Section 6: Independence from the rat race and Bliss

6.1 The Idea of Independence from the rat race

Characterizing independence from the rat race and its association with bliss.

Adjusting the quest for monetary objectives with present bliss.

6.2 The Job of Care in Monetary Bliss

Integrating care rehearses into monetary independent direction.

Developing a feeling of appreciation and happiness in the monetary excursion.

This section investigates the complex connection among cash and satisfaction. From grasping the effect of pay on prosperity to the job of time, connections, and deliberate spending, per users will acquire experiences into how monetary decisions can add to a satisfying and happy life. The section urges a comprehensive way to deal with joy that goes past material belongings and underscores the significance of careful monetary practices.

Cash Mentality

Part 1: Unloading Cash Outlook

1.1 Characterizing Cash Outlook

Investigating the idea of cash outlook and its impact on monetary ways of behaving.

Perceiving the influence of attitude in molding one's relationship with cash.

1.2 The Beginnings of Cash Convictions

Researching how youth encounters and social impacts add to cash attitude.

Distinguishing and grasping instilled cash convictions.

Section 2: Shortage versus Overflow Mentality

2.1 World view limited by fear

Inspecting the effect of a viewpoint that everything is limited on monetary independent direction.

Procedures for perceiving and defeating shortage thinking.

2.2 Developing Overflow

Figuring out the standards of an overflow attitude.

Pragmatic activities to cultivate a mentality of overflow in monetary issues.

Part 3: Fixed versus Development Outlook in Money

3.1 Fixed Outlook

Investigating the constraints of a proper mentality in monetary undertakings.

How a proper outlook can prevent monetary development and flexibility.

3.2 Sustaining a Development Outlook

The advantages of embracing a development outlook in moving toward monetary difficulties.

Procedures for fostering an outlook zeroed in on learning and improvement.

Section 4: Cash and Self-esteem

4.1 The Association Among Cash and Confidence

Analyzing what monetary achievement or battles mean for self-esteem.

Methodologies for decoupling confidence from monetary status.

4.2 Structure a Solid Self-esteem Establishment

Developing a positive mental self view paying little heed to monetary conditions.

Offsetting self-esteem with monetary accomplishments.

Part 5: Overcoming Limiting Beliefs

5.1 Identifying Money-Related Limiting Beliefs Identifying common money-related limiting beliefs.

How these convictions can prevent monetary development.

5.2 Changing Cash Accounts

Procedures for testing and rethinking restricting cash convictions.

Making enabling stories that help monetary achievement.

Section 6: Careful Cash The executives

6.1 Care in Monetary Navigation

Coordinating care rehearses into ordinary monetary decisions.

how mindfulness reduces impulsive behavior and increases awareness.

6.2 Adjusting Cash Activities to Values

The significance of adjusting monetary choices to individual qualities.

Making a monetary arrangement that mirrors one's qualities and yearnings.

This section dives into the domain of cash mentality, investigating the convictions and perspectives that shape our monetary ways of behaving. From understanding the beginnings of cash convictions to developing an overflow attitude and conquering restricting convictions, peruses will acquire bits of knowledge into the strong impact of outlook on monetary prosperity. Reasonable procedures and activities are given to assist people with fostering a positive and development situated cash mentality.

Propensities for Saving and Spending

Part 1: Understanding Propensities for Burning through

1.1 The Brain science of Expenditure Analyzing the profound and mental variables that impact spending designs

What individual characteristics and social means for shape spending approaches to acting.

1.2 Inspiration Spending and Its Consequences

Seeing the impact of rash spending on financial prosperity.

techniques for forestalling indiscreet buys and empowering capable spending.

Segment 2: Arranging as a Foundation

2.1 The Meaning of Arranging

Describing the occupation of arranging in achieving money related targets.

experimenting with various budgeting methods before choosing the one that works best for you. 2.2 Create a Reasonable Spending Plan Reasonable steps for creating a spending plan in light of pay, costs, and financial goals.

modifying and adhering to the long-term financial plan.

Part 3: Savvy Saving Approaches

3.1 The Justification behind Saving Making sense of the various purposes behind saving money.

Objective setting as a motivation for unsurprising saving affinities.

3.2 Successful Saving Methodologies Researching

different reserve funds procedures like computerized investment funds and rate based investment funds.

Beating obstacles to standard saving and building a speculation supports standpoint.

Area 4: Needs versus Needs

4.1 Perceiving Endlessly needs

Getting a handle on the difference between principal costs and discretionary spending.

Zeroing in on needs while at this point thinking about needs in a fair financial plan.

4.2 Insightful Commercialization

Taking on an insightful method for managing spending that lines up with individual characteristics.

Chasing after intentional choices to help affordable and critical usage.

Part 5: Lifestyle Extension and Its Entrapments

5.1 The Catch of Lifestyle Extension

Perceiving the dangers of extending getting a charge out of couple with pay.

Methods for avoiding lifestyle development and staying aware of financial discipline.

5.2 Changing Joy and Financial Goals

Finding a concordance between participating in life's delights and setting something to the side for what's to come.

integrating optional spending without endangering monetary objectives as long as possible.

Area 6: 6.1 The Importance of Emergency Funds

Recognizing the significance of emergency funds Creating and maintaining a sufficient emergency fund

6.2 Construction Financial Adaptability

Methodology for arranging financially for unexpected expenses or money related droops.

The psychological benefits of having a money related security net.

This segment dives into the intricacies of use and saving affinities, offering pieces of information into the psychological pieces of financial choices. From understanding the motivations driving spending to practical arranging techniques and the meaning of building save reserves, per users will secure gadgets and strategies to develop better money related approaches to acting. The part in like manner tends to the agreement among necessities and requirements, mindful industrialism, and the significance of emergency resources for financial adaptability.

Psychology and Investing:

Chapter 1: Feelings and financial planning

1.1 The Profound Rollercoaster of Financial planning

Investigating the profound ups and downs experienced by financial backers.

Grasping the effect of feelings on venture choices.

1.2 Ability to understand people at their core in Financial planning

The job of the ability to understand people on a deeper level in exploring the vulnerabilities of the market.

Creating mindfulness and profound guideline for better venture results.

Section 2: Conduct Predispositions in Speculation Choices

2.1 Mental Predispositions in Effective money management

Perceiving normal mental inclinations that impact speculation decisions.

How predispositions can prompt less than ideal speculation procedures.

2.2 Overcoming Bias in Investment Strategies for mitigating cognitive bias and making investment decisions that are more rational.

The significance of expansion and restrained navigation.

Part 3: Risk Resilience and Chance Insight

3.1 Figuring out Hazard Resilience

Evaluating individual gamble resilience and its effect on speculation systems.

Adjusting chance and return with regards to monetary objectives.

3.2 Behavioral Aspects of Risk Perception How investment risk

perception is influenced by psychological factors.

Systems for adjusting risk insight to genuine gamble evaluations.

Section 4: Financial backer Conduct in Market Patterns

4.1 Group Mindset and Market Patterns

Investigating the effect of crowd conduct on speculation patterns.

Exploring market bubbles and staying away from speculative snares.

Methodologies for autonomous reasoning even with market feeling.

Part 5: 5.1 The Power of Patience Having a Long-Term

Perspective Understanding the psychological challenges of Long-Term Investing

The intensifying impact and the significance of keeping with it.

5.2 Conquering Short-Termism

Methodologies for defeating the mental tension of momentary market changes.

Zeroing in on basics and keeping an essential venture skyline.

Section 6: Financial backer Attitude in Unpredictable Business sectors

6.1 Adapting to Market Instability

Mental systems for overseeing pressure during times of market unpredictability.

The job of training and data in quieting speculation nerves.

6.2 Transforming Difficulties into Open doors

Seeing business sector slumps as any open doors for vital speculation.

cultivating a resilient mindset to navigate financial market ups and downs.

This section dives into the brain research of money management, tending to the close to home and mental variables that impact speculation choices. From understanding inclinations and hazard discernment to investigating the effect of market patterns and the significance of a drawn out viewpoint, peruses will acquire experiences into the mental parts of fruitful money management. In addition, practical strategies for controlling emotions, reducing biases, and maintaining a resilient mindset in the face of market volatility are provided in this chapter.

Money related Planning and Goal Setting

Section 1: The Meaning of Financial Arrangement

1.1 The Occupation of Financial Arrangement All through regular day to day existence

Portraying financial arrangement and its significance for individuals and families.

Grasping the complete thought of financial readiness past preparation.

1.2 Establish Important Strengths for an Organization Establishing the Foundations of a Strong Financial Institution

The connection between general prosperity and financial security.

Segment 2: Defining Monetary Objectives

That Are Explicit, Quantifiable, Attainable, Pertinent, and Time-

Bound (Brilliant) Presenting the Savvy rules for objective setting
How Splendid goals add to convincing financial readiness.

2.2 Distinctive Individual Financial Goals
Frameworks for recognizing and zeroing in on individual financial goals.

Changing present second and long stretch targets with individual characteristics.

Part 3: Fostering an Individual Spending plan

3.1 Planning as a Monetary Control Instrument Understanding the job that planning plays in accomplishing monetary goals

Sensible steps for making a modified spending plan.

3.2 Anticipating Store assets and Adventures

Appropriating resources for hold assets, adventures, and commitment repayment reasonable.

Balancing discretionary getting a charge out of with financial goals.

Area 4: Commitment The board Approaches

4.1 Getting a handle on Commitment's Impact on Money related Goals

Checking out at the association among commitment and money related flourishing.

Frameworks for supervising and taking care of past responsibilities effectively.

4.2 Defining Objectives for Being Without obligation Laying out goals for becoming obligation free and the mental benefits of obligation decrease

Making a course of action to deal with commitment effectively.

Part 5: Adventure Orchestrating

5.1 The Meaning of Interest in Laying out areas of strength for an establishment

Sorting out the gig of interests in long stretch financial accomplishment.

in speculation arranging, risk the board and broadening.

Evaluating risk versatility and time horizon for different goals.

Area 6: Retirement Organizing

6.1 The Importance of Retirement Organizing

Seeing the meaning of making game plans for retirement.

Approaches for spreading out and achieving retirement speculation finances targets.

6.2 Investigating Advantages Plans and Government upheld retirement

Understanding the occupation of advantages plans and Government moved retirement in retirement organizing.

Intensifying benefits and choosing informed decisions about retirement pay sources.

Part 7: Typical Overview and Change

7.1 The Influential Thought of Financial Arrangement

Underlining the necessity for standard reviews and changes in financial plans.

Acclimating to changes in life conditions, targets, and financial conditions.

7.2 Searching for Capable Heading

Knowing when to search for help from money related specialists.

The value of joint exertion in achieving complex financial objectives.

This part gives a broad manual for financial planning and goal setting. From sorting out the meaning of money related aiming to characterizing Clever goals, making monetary arrangements, directing commitment, and expecting retirement, pursuers will secure feasible encounters and approaches for achieving their financial cravings. The part emphasizes the influential thought of money related readiness, enabling standard reviews and acclimations to ensure plan with creating life conditions and targets.

Money and Associations

Area 1: The Interconnection of Money and Associations

1.1 Seeing the Impact of Assets on Associations

Investigating what money related components can mean for the strength of associations.

understanding the likely reasons for monetary pressure.

1.2 The Occupation of Correspondence as one

Focusing on the meaning of straightforward correspondence about cash.

Strategies for encouraging valuable monetary discussions in connections.

Segment 2: Shared Values and Money related Closeness

2.1 Distinctive Shared Money related Characteristics

Grasping the importance of shared values in money related route.

deciding if monetary mentalities and needs are viable.

2.2 Investigating Differentiations in Financial Perspectives

Methods for supervising and associating openings in financial perspectives.

Choosing something that would merit settling on and set out some reasonable compromise in financial issues.

Part 3: Money related Readiness collectively

3.1 The Upsides of Joint Financial Readiness

Researching the potential gains of helpful money related planning in associations.

Judicious steps for making joint financial targets and plans.

3.2 Changing Opportunity and Relationship

Staying aware of individual money related characters while developing a sensation of partnership.

Strategies for finding a concordance between money related opportunity and shared liabilities.

Area 4: Money and Relationship Accomplishments

4.1 Investigating Financial Accomplishments Together

Watching out for the impact of huge life changing circumstances (e.g., marriage, buying a home, having children) on reserves.

Anticipating and directing money related changes during immense life propels.

4.2 Long stretch Financial Arrangement all things considered

Setting and seeking after long stretch financial targets collectively. The occupation of normal assistance in achieving shared money related targets.

Part 5: Conquering Relationship Monetary Snags

5.1 Adapting to Monetary Pressure

Procedures for Overseeing Relationship Monetary Pressure

The meaning of consistent encouragement and cooperation in attempting monetary times.

5.2 Settling Money related Battles

Convincing correspondence methodology for settling conflicts associated with cash.

Searching for set out some reasonable compromise and finding game plans that benefit the two assistants.

Area 6: Financial Opportunity and Autonomy

6.1 Changing Independence and Joint Financial Goals

Methods for staying aware of individual financial opportunity inside a typical money related structure.

Advancing both individual monetary turn of events and aggregate monetary achievement.

6.2 Cooperative Navigation The financial advantages of a cooperative dynamic

Investigating major financial decisions through open talk and normal plan.

This part researches the erratic association among money and associations. The reader will gain insight into the process of building solid, adaptable financial organizations by learning about everything from the impact of money on relationship components to effective communication strategies, shared financial preparation, and analyzing successes and challenges. Additionally, the section offers couples who want to achieve both their own and each other's financial goals practical guidance on how to achieve this balance.

Adjusting to Financial Tension

Segment 1: Figuring out Monetary Pressure

1.1 Perceiving Monetary Pressure

Marks of Monetary Pressure

Normal monetary pressure pointers

Understanding how financial tension can show up in various pieces of life.

1.2 How Money Affects Prosperity

Examining the mental and physical effects of prolonged financial stress.

recognizing the connection between general prosperity and financial health.

Segment 2: Procedures for Guaranteed Relief

2.1 Crisis Financial Preparation

Making a temporary financial arrangement to deal with immediate stressors

Zeroing in on central expenses and finding short lived game plans.

2.2 Seeking Assistance Establish a supportive group of individuals to discuss issues and seek direction.

utilizing services for financial advice and group assets.

Part 3: 3.1 Care Practices for Monetary

Pressure Presents care procedures for overseeing pressure right now. Care and Stress Decrease

Incorporating care into regular timetables for long stretch advantages.

3.2 Stress-Relieving Exercises Identifying and participating in activities that promote relaxation and stress reduction

The occupation of dealing with oneself in staying aware of significant flourishing during financial troubles.

Area 4: Building Monetary Versatility

4.1 Structure Monetary Versatility Methods for Creating Flexibility Despite Financial Misfortunes

Fostering a positive mindset and flexible financial approaches to acting.

4.2 Acquiring from Troubles

Isolating delineations from money related difficulties to enlighten future autonomous course.

Considering troubles to be any entryways for individual and money related advancement.

Part 5: Communicating about Financial Stress

5.1 Open Communication in Relationships The significance of open communication regarding financial stress within relationships.

Strategies for beginning conversations and conveying concerns accommodatingly.

5.2 Searching for Capable Course

The occupation of financial aides and consultants in investigating money related pressure.

collaborating with experts to create significant financial improvement plans.

Area 6: Long stretch Money related Wellbeing

6.1 Spreading out Money related Targets for Recovery

Spreading out functional and reachable money related goals to seek after.

The influential power of having a somewhat long financial vision.

6.2 Monetary Schooling and strengthening The commitment that continuous monetary instruction makes to the improvement of confidence and flexibility

Empowering individuals to accept control over their money related future.

This segment gives techniques and pieces of information to adjusting to financial tension. Peruses will procure apparatuses for exploring troublesome monetary circumstances, for example, prompt help measures, care works on, building monetary flexibility, and empowering open correspondence. The segment furthermore emphasizes the meaning of searching for capable heading when required and includes the long pieces of money related wellbeing, engaging individuals to spread out targets and continue with their financial tutoring for upheld thriving.

Case Studies and Examples from the Real World Chapter

1: 1.1 Inspecting Individual Monetary

Excursions Introducing genuine instances of people or families who have made monetary progress.

Taking the main illustrations and techniques from their encounters.

1.2 Perceiving Ordinary Subjects

Separating divided attributes between different instances of beating difficulty.

Understanding the norms and approaches to acting that add to money related success.

Segment 2: Investigating Financial Troubles through Relevant examinations

2.1 Sorting out Arranged Financial Hardships

Presenting logical examinations that highlight an extent of money related troubles.

Taking a gander at the surprising strategies individuals used to beat hardship.

2.2 Strategies for Adaptability and Recovery

Removing models on strength and recovery from testing money related conditions.

Recognizing instances of productive strategy for practical adaptations.

Part 3: Lead Encounters from Authentic Models

3.1 Dumping Individual lead guidelines

Looking at authentic advisers for appreciate typical individual lead guidelines in financial course.

how mental preferences and emotions affect decisions that can be proven.

3.2 Approaches for Lead Change

Isolating sober minded methods for individuals expecting to change their financial approaches to acting. Applying social monetary issues thoughts to veritable circumstances.

Area 4: Relevant examinations in Financial Readiness and Objective Achievement

4.1 Objective Achievement

Instances of conquering misfortune Presenting relevant examinations of individuals who really cultivated their financial targets.

recognizing the effective systems for arranging and completing them.

4.2 Overcoming Obstacles in Objective Pursuit

Examining instances in which individuals encountered obstacles in objective pursuit

Systems for beating unexpected obstructions and adjusting to them.

Part 5: 5.1 Breaking down Monetary

Errors Contextual investigations that feature normal monetary slip-ups made by people.

removing examples and information about how to avoid similar traps.

5.2 Changing Stumbles into Open entryways

Philosophies for individuals to change financial slips up into astonishing entryways for advancement.

Fostering a positive and proactive mindset despite troubles.

Area 6: Relevant examinations In real money and Associations

6.1 Powerful Money related Affiliations

Relevant investigations of couples or families who have investigated money related hardships actually.

removing examples of successful collaboration and correspondence.

6.2 Watching out for Financial Strain in Associations

Certifiable cases of couples beating money related strain.

Methodology for developing financial adaptability and keeping with sound associations.

This section digs into true contextual investigations to give substantial instances of individuals' monetary excursions, troubles, victories, and procedures. People can learn a lot about both positive and challenging financial situations by looking at a variety of situations. The subjects canvassed in this part range from standards of conduct and accomplishing objectives to gaining from botches and exploring connections' monetary elements. Each logical examination fills in as a practical blueprint, offering models and inspiration for pursuers on their own financial outings.

End

In the excursion through the different features of individual budget, we've investigated the complexities of cash the board, the brain science behind monetary choices, and the significant effect of funds on connections. From understanding the nuts and bolts of planning and reserve funds to digging into the mind boggling domains of money management and social financial matters, this investigation has expected to furnish you with information and procedures to explore the different difficulties and open doors in your monetary life.

Key Learning:

Monetary Health is Comprehensive: Accomplishing monetary prosperity reaches out past simple planning or effective money management. It includes grasping the profound and mental parts of cash, defining significant objectives, and supporting solid monetary propensities.

Mentality Matters: Your convictions and mentalities toward cash can altogether impact your monetary results. Developing a positive cash outlook and monitoring mental inclinations can enable you to go with additional educated choices.

Connections and Cash are Interconnected: The elements of cash inside connections can influence the general wellbeing of organizations. Open correspondence, shared values, and cooperative monetary arranging are critical for keeping up with monetary congruity.

Flexibility Notwithstanding Difficulties: Failures in finances are a part of life. Getting over obstacles and moving forward necessitates acquiring financial resiliency, learning from mistakes, and seeking assistance when needed.

Objective Setting and Arranging are Critical: Laying out clear, feasible monetary objectives and making an insightful arrangement to contact them structure the groundwork of monetary achievement. Normal surveys and changes guarantee that your monetary arrangement stays lined up with your advancing life conditions.

Ceaseless Learning and Variation: The monetary scene is steadily advancing. Long-term financial success is aided by staying informed, adapting to changes, and seeking ongoing personal finance education.

As you proceed with your monetary excursion, recall that everybody's way is extraordinary, and there's nobody size-fits-all arrangement. Your monetary objectives, conditions, and values are unmistakable, and your way to deal with cash ought to mirror that singularity.

Furnished with the bits of knowledge acquired from this investigation, you have the instruments to pursue informed choices, develop a positive monetary mentality, and explore the intricacies of your monetary scene. Whether you're pursuing independence from the rat race, trying to beat difficulties, or essentially taking a stab at a decent and satisfying monetary life, the excursion is continuous. Embrace the growing experience, commend your triumphs, and stay strong despite affliction.

May your monetary excursion be one of development, strengthening, and at last, a wellspring of happiness and prosperity in your life.